MW01005961

PROGRESS JOURNAL

A Simple Daily Planner and Productivity Tracker to Make Meaningful Progress on Your Most Important Work

***

Nick Loper

Copyright and Disclaimer

Introduction

"What gets measured gets managed."

-Peter Drucker

*****

You can see the brake lights up ahead so you begin to slow down.

Before long, all 4 lanes are moving at a crawl. The speed limit sign taunts you with its audacious 65 mph suggestion. You could walk faster than this!

Even worse, you can't see past the SUV in front of you, so you have no idea how long the traffic jam goes on for—or what is causing it. You're stuck; trapped, and powerless to do anything about it.

When I used to commute to my old job, I would often take the winding, empty, country road home. It was a longer and slower route—that is, assuming there was no traffic on the freeway.

I chose that route because it was consistent. Even if it was slower some days, I made steady progress toward my destination. I never once felt trapped or powerless or wanting to scream obscenities through the windshield.

In building a number of businesses over the last 15 years, I realize I've made the same choice: steady, dedicated, consistent progress, over the "fast lane" or "shiny object" alternatives.

In *The Slight Edge*, author Jeff Olson defines success as **"the progressive realization of a worthy ideal."**

The "progressive realization" part is key; success is a cumulative, consistent process, not an overnight lucky break.

The Problem

Ever feel stuck or stagnant?

You're busy, but are you really seeing results from your efforts?

Are you moving forward, or just treading water?

It's frustrating, and frankly, it's exhausting.

But how do you know what to work on?

The problem is that many of the things that create success in the long run, don't look like they're having any impact at all in the short run.

If you go to the gym today, you're not going to have a six-pack tomorrow. And similarly, if you don't go to the gym today, you're not going to keel over from obesity tomorrow.

So we end up scattered and inconsistent, with no real plan.

We're easily distracted and at the end of our days and weeks, we don't have a great answer for what we really accomplished.

Is that how you want to live? Just going through the motions?

Instead, I'll propose a simple but purposeful way to plan out your most important work—and track your results—so that your effort is never wasted.

The Solution

In an effort to squeeze more results out of my limited hours, I've studied productivity and efficiency for years. I've tried just about every productivity "hack" out there—everything from cold showers to supposed focus-enhancing music and "smart" drugs.

While those experiments were fun and interesting (and perhaps mildly successful), the most surprising thing I've found is that just **a handful of keystone habits** tend to make the biggest impact on my personal productivity.

Those are the habits I've baked into this journal, and the ones I'm confident will have you feeling better and more productive about your work right away.

Those keystone habits, as you'll see in the following pages, are:

- Setting short-term "sprint" goals, and breaking those down into the smallest actionable steps.
- Identifying your top 1-3 priorities each day and measuring your progress on those.
- Practicing gratitude.
- Establishing and tracking too-small-to-fail "micro habits".
- Identifying and tracking your Key Performance Indicators.

If it sounds like a lot to do, don't worry. I'll break down how to do each of those in the next section.

It's not a huge time commitment or massive lifestyle shift. In fact, using this journal should take **less than 5 minutes a day.**

And based on my experience and interviews with hundreds of successful entrepreneurs, it's 5 minutes well spent.

Why Me?

When I was a kid, my favorite video games were the ones you could save and return to your quest or season later.

The Legend of Zelda.

Base Wars.

Ken Griffey Jr.'s Major League Baseball.

Other bloggers publish income reports; I publish progress reports.

I'm obsessed with progress.

(If you're curious, you can read them at sidehustlenation.com/progress-reports.)

To me, progress means forward motion, or actively taking the steps to improve each day. It's one thing we can control.

And progress is universal; everyone can make progress toward their goals in some meaningful way, however small the steps may seem.

It turns out I'm not alone either. We're wired to seek progress; psychologists have found it to be a key factor in our overall happiness.

Even Tony Robbins calls it the "1-word secret to happiness," telling CNBC, "I always tell people if you want to know the secret to happiness, I can give it to you in one word: progress."

My Guarantee

If you follow the guidelines and prompts in this journal, I guarantee you'll feel more satisfied and productive with your work after just 28 days.

If you don't, just send me a note (my contact info is at the end of the book), and I'll buy the journal back from you, no questions asked.

Now, where else are you going to find a deal like that?

Ready? Let's get started!

Claim Your Free Bonuses

In the spirit of improving not just your productivity, but your overall effectiveness, I put together an exclusive bonus package for users of *The Progress Journal.*

1. The Productivity Tip Sheet

I asked some of my most successful entrepreneurial friends for their favorite productivity tips and tricks.

The result is this Tip Sheet.

I don't expect you to try all of these—especially not all at once—but use the quick-to-implement suggestions on this list to re-energize and re-focus.

2. The Digital Progress Journal

Several readers requested a digital version of the journal to use with their tablet and stylus. If you're embracing a paperless lifestyle, this one is for you.

Plus, it includes two extra 4-week blocks.

Grab them both free here:

ProgressJournal.net/bonus

How to Use This Journal

This journal is structured in four 4-week blocks. This is intentional—you don't have to wait for an arbitrary flip of the calendar to start using it.

You can think of these time blocks as project "sprints" or dedicated periods to make progress on one specific goal.

The four 4-week blocks represent about a third of a year's worth of tracking, but you do *not* have to use them consecutively.

The pages and prompts don't expire. Begin a time block whenever you're ready.

(Of course, I think once you get going, you'll want to *keep* going.)

The Block Level

Each block lasts 4 weeks. At the beginning of each of these, you'll decide on your primary goal for the next 28 days.

Goal Setting 101

You're probably already familiar with the idea of setting SMART goals, but if not, here's how it works.

SMART goals are:

Specific – Cast aside vague goals like "grow my business" in favor of specific ones like "land 5 new website clients," "launch my book," or "make an extra $2000."

Measurable – How will you know if you achieved your goal? By giving a concrete result.

Instead of goals like "eat healthier" or "lose weight," SMART goals sound like "eat 5 servings of vegetables a day," or "lose 10 pounds."

Achievable – Make your goals ambitious but attainable.

Relevant – Your goals should reflect something important to you and your business. Otherwise, what's the point?

Time-bound – Your goals in this journal are naturally time-bound by the 28-day blocks, but if you have longer goals in mind, be sure to assign them a deadline as well.

Having a destination in mind is crucial. Where do you want to go? What do you want to get done?

Key Supporting Tasks

After you set your primary goal for the time block, I want you to break down that goal into its smallest actionable steps.

For instance, if my goal is to launch a new book, I'd have key supporting tasks like:

- Complete outline or mind map.
- Complete rough draft.
- Find and hire an editor.
- Format the final version for ebook and paperback.
- Create a cover design.
- Recruit a launch team.
- Record the audiobook or hire a narrator.
- Upload to Amazon.

Of course, these will vary depending on your goal, but it's important to map out the action steps you'll need to take to get there.

Plus, these smaller action steps will help dictate your daily priorities to help you stay focused and make meaningful progress.

Micro Habit Tracking

When I'm trying to develop new habits or experiment with new ideas, one thing I've found helpful is to set up what I call a "micro habit"—and challenge myself to do it for 30 days.

You've probably seen challenges like Whole30, in which participants can only eat certain healthy foods for 30 days.

Micro habits aren't meant to be that extreme or lifestyle-changing, but I think you'll find they can be gateways, or triggers, to larger habits.

These habits should take 5 minutes or less, and the idea is to make them "too-small-to-fail."

Here are some examples:

- Do 10 pushups
- Floss
- Meditate
- Drink a glass of water first thing in the morning
- Express gratitude
- Make a cold call
- Write down one new product idea
- Reconnect with an old friend or client

Your micro habits definitely don't need to be 100% business-related. In fact, I usually have a mixture of health, business, and relationship habits I'm working on.

Each 28-day block will ask you for 2-4 micro habits to track. You can keep the same ones for each block, or change it up and try new ones.

The Week Level

At the end of each week, you'll fill in a prompt for what you're most proud of. What went well?

You'll also have an opportunity to describe any obstacles or resistance you faced, and to note where you can improve for the following week.

The Progress Bar

Each weekly review page also has a "progress bar" that looks like this:

0%   50%   100%

This is to give you a visual representation of how well you're tracking toward your primary goal for the time block.

Just color it in up to the point of progress you estimate you've made, like this:

0%   50%   100%

The Day Level

Each day, the journal will ask what you got done. It's very straightforward; simply fill in this section with the work you did that day.

The idea here is to celebrate and recognize the small tasks that get you closer to your goal.

Plus, your daily "this is what I got done" tracking will give you a feel for where your working hours are really going and build satisfaction in your consistent effort and progress.

Gratitude Journaling

This journal also includes an opportunity to track what you're grateful for each day.

A consistent gratitude habit has been linked to improved emotional and physical health, better sleep, and greater overall happiness.

Tomorrow's Priorities

Instead of waking up and wondering what to work on, avoid wasting time and energy by naming your top 1-3 priorities for tomorrow each night.

That way, you know exactly what to tackle when you get to work.

Micro Habit Tracking

Each daily journal page also has a series of checkboxes for you to input your chosen micro habits and whether or not you got them done that day.

Your Key Performance Indicators

Before you begin, take a moment to think about the key performance indicators (KPIs) in your life or business.

These are the metrics that have the biggest impact on your overall operation.

In my business, for example, the primary KPIs I track are:

- Email subscribers
- Podcast downloads
- Website traffic

One reader recently asked me, "Well, isn't profit the only real KPI that matters?"

And while I agree that profit is important—the business can't survive without it—and it is something I track almost daily, I've found it to be a lagging indicator compared to these other metrics.

What I mean by that is if I can get those other numbers to increase, the profit will follow.

Your KPIs are the levers you can pull on to create real change.

What Makes a Good KPI?

The best KPIs have two characteristics in common.

First, they are numbers you have influence over. It might not be easy, but with effort, you can change them.

Second, they make a meaningful impact on your bottom line or quality of life.

Let's look at some examples.

If you're an Uber driver, the price of gas directly impacts your profitability, but it's not something you have any control over—so it doesn't make a great KPI.

Instead, it might make more sense to track the number of hours driven, the number of "surge" rides, or your effective hourly rate.

If you're a freelancer, the two things you're paying most attention to are the flow of quality leads coming across your desk, and your ability to deliver results to clients.

In terms of KPIs, you might decide to track discovery calls, proposals sent, or average job value. These are things you have direct control over and will make a meaningful impact to your business.

In e-commerce, you might track your cost to acquire a new customer, the lifetime value of a customer, or your conversion rate.

Changeable and impactful.

In determining your KPIs, consider the focusing question from *The ONE Thing*:

"What's the ONE Thing I can do right now such that by doing it everything else will be easier or unnecessary?"

Choosing Your KPIs

Each business is different. The numbers that matter most to you might be:

- New client leads
- Words written
- Sales
- Designs submitted
- Conversion rate
- Cost per lead
- Revenue per pageview
- Profit margin
- Net promoter score
- Average order value
- Hours billed to clients

One friend of mine counts "thank you cards received" as one of his most important KPIs. His reasoning is if his work is strong enough to receive unsolicited thank you notes in the mail, he's obviously making a positive impact.

Your Baseline

Let's get a baseline for where you're at today.

Pick 3-5 KPIs and make a note of your current performance on those.

For example, if I was filling this section in today, I would put something like this:

1. **Email Subscribers** – 68,000; growing at roughly 50 net new subscribers per day.

2. **Podcast Downloads** – new episodes are reaching 25,000 downloads in the first 30 days.

3. **Website Traffic** – 138,000 visitors over the last 30 days.

Fill in the section below with your "starting point" KPIs.

1. _____

   _____

2. _____

   _____

3. _____

   _____

4. _____

   _____

5. _____

   _____

Ready to begin your first block? Let's do it!

Block 1

My primary goal for the next 4 weeks is ...

_____

_____

What are the key supporting tasks I need to get done to make that goal a reality? Break it down into the smallest actionable steps.

_____

_____

_____

_____

_____

_____

_____

_____

What 2-4 micro habits will I track over the next 4 weeks?

1. _____

2. _____

3. _____

4. _____

Where will I start? What are my top 1-3 priorities for tomorrow?

1. _____

2. _____

3. _____

Day 1: _____ (fill in the date)

What did I get done today?

_____

_____

_____

_____

What am I grateful for?

_____

_____

_____

What are my top 1-3 priorities for tomorrow?	Micro habit tracker
1. _____	☐ _____
	☐ _____
2. _____	☐ _____
	☐ _____
3. _____	☐ _____

Day 2: _____

What did I get done today?

_____

_____

_____

_____

What am I grateful for?

_____

_____

_____

What are my top 1-3 priorities for tomorrow?

1. _____

2. _____

3. _____

Micro habit tracker

☐ _____

☐ _____

☐ _____

☐ _____

Day 3: _____

What did I get done today?

_____

_____

_____

_____

What am I grateful for?

_____

_____

_____

What are my top 1-3 priorities for tomorrow?	Micro habit tracker
1. _____	☐ _____
	☐ _____
2. _____	☐ _____
3. _____	☐ _____

Day 4: _____

What did I get done today?

_____

_____

_____

_____

What am I grateful for?

_____

_____

_____

What are my top 1-3 priorities for tomorrow?

Micro habit tracker

1. _____   ☐ _____

☐ _____

2. _____   ☐ _____

3. _____   ☐ _____

Day 5: _____

What did I get done today?

_____

_____

_____

_____

What am I grateful for?

_____

_____

_____

What are my top 1-3 priorities for tomorrow?	Micro habit tracker
1. _____	☐ _____
2. _____	☐ _____
	☐ _____
3. _____	☐ _____

Day 6: _____

What did I get done today?

_____

_____

_____

_____

What am I grateful for?

_____

_____

_____

What are my top 1-3
priorities for tomorrow?

Micro habit tracker

1. _____

☐ _____

☐ _____

2. _____

☐ _____

3. _____

☐ _____

Day 7: _____

What did I get done today?

_____

_____

_____

_____

What am I grateful for?

_____

_____

_____

What are my top 1-3 priorities for tomorrow?	Micro habit tracker
1. _____	☐ _____
	☐ _____
2. _____	☐ _____
	☐ _____
3. _____	☐ _____

Week 1 Review

What am I most proud of this week?

_____

_____

_____

What obstacles or resistance did I face? Where can I improve?

_____

_____

_____

_____

_____

How am I tracking toward my 4-week goal? Shade in the progress bar below:

0%	50%	100%

Day 8: _____

What did I get done today?

_____

_____

_____

_____

What am I grateful for?

_____

_____

_____

What are my top 1-3 priorities for tomorrow?

1. _____

2. _____

3. _____

Micro habit tracker

☐ _____

☐ _____

☐ _____

☐ _____

Day 9: _____

What did I get done today?

_____

_____

_____

_____

What am I grateful for?

_____

_____

_____

What are my top 1-3 priorities for tomorrow?	Micro habit tracker
1. _____	☐ _____
	☐ _____
2. _____	☐ _____
3. _____	☐ _____

Day 10: _____

What did I get done today?

_____

_____

_____

_____

What am I grateful for?

_____

_____

_____

What are my top 1-3 priorities for tomorrow?	Micro habit tracker
1. _____	☐ _____
	☐ _____
2. _____	☐ _____
3. _____	☐ _____

Day 11: _____

What did I get done today?

_____

_____

_____

_____

What am I grateful for?

_____

_____

_____

What are my top 1-3 priorities for tomorrow?

1. _____

2. _____

3. _____

Micro habit tracker

☐ _____

☐ _____

☐ _____

☐ _____

Day 12: _____

What did I get done today?

_____

_____

_____

_____

What am I grateful for?

_____

_____

_____

What are my top 1-3 priorities for tomorrow?

Micro habit tracker

1. _____

2. _____

3. _____

☐ _____

☐ _____

☐ _____

☐ _____

Day 13: _____

What did I get done today?

_____

_____

_____

_____

What am I grateful for?

_____

_____

_____

What are my top 1-3 priorities for tomorrow?

Micro habit tracker

1. _____   ☐ _____

2. _____   ☐ _____
                      ☐ _____
3. _____   ☐ _____

Day 14: _____

What did I get done today?

_____

_____

_____

_____

What am I grateful for?

_____

_____

_____

What are my top 1-3 priorities for tomorrow?

1. _____

2. _____

3. _____

Micro habit tracker

☐ _____

☐ _____

☐ _____

☐ _____

Week 2 Review

What am I most proud of this week?

_____

_____

What obstacles or resistance did I face? Where can I improve?

_____

_____

_____

_____

_____

How am I tracking toward my 4-week goal? Shade in the progress bar below:

0%	50%	100%

Day 15: _____

What did I get done today?

_____

_____

_____

_____

What am I grateful for?

_____

_____

_____

What are my top 1-3 priorities for tomorrow?   Micro habit tracker

1. _____   ☐ _____

                            ☐ _____

2. _____   ☐ _____

                            ☐ _____

3. _____   ☐ _____

Day 16: _____

What did I get done today?

_____

_____

_____

_____

What am I grateful for?

_____

_____

_____

What are my top 1-3 priorities for tomorrow?	Micro habit tracker
1. _____	☐ _____
2. _____	☐ _____
	☐ _____
3. _____	☐ _____

Day 17: _____

What did I get done today?

_____

_____

_____

_____

What am I grateful for?

_____

_____

_____

What are my top 1-3
priorities for tomorrow?

Micro habit tracker

1. _____   ☐ _____

☐ _____

2. _____   ☐ _____

3. _____   ☐ _____

Day 18: _____

What did I get done today?

_____

_____

_____

_____

What am I grateful for?

_____

_____

_____

What are my top 1-3 priorities for tomorrow?

Micro habit tracker

1. _____   ☐ _____

☐ _____

2. _____   ☐ _____

3. _____   ☐ _____

Day 19: _____

What did I get done today?

_____

_____

_____

_____

What am I grateful for?

_____

_____

_____

What are my top 1-3 priorities for tomorrow?

1. _____

2. _____

3. _____

Micro habit tracker

☐ _____

☐ _____

☐ _____

☐ _____

Day 20: _____

What did I get done today?

_____

_____

_____

_____

What am I grateful for?

_____

_____

_____

What are my top 1-3 priorities for tomorrow?

Micro habit tracker

1. _____   ☐ _____

☐ _____

2. _____   ☐ _____

☐ _____

3. _____

Day 21: _____

What did I get done today?

_____

_____

_____

_____

What am I grateful for?

_____

_____

_____

What are my top 1-3 priorities for tomorrow?	Micro habit tracker
1. _____	☐ _____
	☐ _____
2. _____	☐ _____
	☐ _____
3. _____	☐ _____

Week 3 Review

What am I most proud of this week?

_____

_____

_____

What obstacles or resistance did I face? Where can I improve?

_____

_____

_____

_____

_____

How am I tracking toward my 4-week goal? Shade in the progress bar below:

0%   50%   100%

Day 22: _____

What did I get done today?

_____

_____

_____

_____

What am I grateful for?

_____

_____

_____

What are my top 1-3 priorities for tomorrow?	Micro habit tracker
1. _____	☐ _____
	☐ _____
2. _____	☐ _____
	☐ _____
3. _____	☐ _____

Day 23: _____

What did I get done today?

_____

_____

_____

_____

What am I grateful for?

_____

_____

_____

What are my top 1-3 priorities for tomorrow?

Micro habit tracker

1. _____

2. _____

3. _____

☐ _____

☐ _____

☐ _____

☐ _____

Day 24: _____

What did I get done today?

_____

_____

_____

_____

What am I grateful for?

_____

_____

_____

What are my top 1-3 priorities for tomorrow?	Micro habit tracker
1. _____	☐ _____
	☐ _____
2. _____	☐ _____
	☐ _____
3. _____	☐ _____

Day 25: _____

What did I get done today?

_____

_____

_____

_____

What am I grateful for?

_____

_____

_____

What are my top 1-3 priorities for tomorrow?

1. _____

2. _____

3. _____

Micro habit tracker

☐ _____

☐ _____

☐ _____

☐ _____

Day 26: _____

What did I get done today?

_____

_____

_____

_____

What am I grateful for?

_____

_____

_____

What are my top 1-3
priorities for tomorrow?

Micro habit tracker

1. _____   ☐ _____

☐ _____

2. _____   ☐ _____

☐ _____

3. _____   ☐ _____

Day 27: _____

What did I get done today?

_____

_____

_____

_____

What am I grateful for?

_____

_____

_____

What are my top 1-3 priorities for tomorrow?

1. _____

2. _____

3. _____

Micro habit tracker

☐ _____

☐ _____

☐ _____

☐ _____

Day 28: _____

What did I get done today?

_____

_____

_____

_____

What am I grateful for?

_____

_____

_____

What are my top 1-3 priorities for tomorrow?	**Micro habit tracker**

1. _____

2. _____

3. _____

☐ _____

☐ _____

☐ _____

☐ _____

Week 4 Review

What am I most proud of this week?

_____

_____

_____

What obstacles or resistance did I face? Where can I improve?

_____

_____

_____

_____

_____

How am I tracking toward my 4-week goal? Shade in the progress bar below:

0%   50%   100%

Block 1 Review

Did I accomplish my primary goal?
☐ Yes!   ☐ No

If no, why not?

_____

_____

_____

What worked well over the last 4 weeks?

_____

_____

_____

How am I tracking on my KPI metrics?

1. _____

_____

2. _____

_____

3. _____

_____

4. _____

_____

5. _____

_____

Was I able to "move the needle" on any Key Performance
Indicators? Why or why not?

_____

_____

_____

_____

_____

Block 2

My primary goal for the next 4 weeks is ...

_____

_____

What are the key supporting tasks I need to get done to make
that goal a reality? Break it down into the smallest actionable
steps.

_____

_____

_____

_____

_____

_____

_____

_____

What 2-4 micro habits will I track over the next 4 weeks?

1. _____

2. _____

3. _____

4. _____

Where will I start? What are my top 1-3 priorities for tomorrow?

1. _____

2. _____

3. _____

Day 1: _____ (fill in the date)

What did I get done today?

_____

_____

_____

_____

What am I grateful for?

_____

_____

_____

What are my top 1-3 priorities for tomorrow?

Micro habit tracker

1. _____   ☐ _____

                       ☐ _____

2. _____   ☐ _____

3. _____   ☐ _____

Day 2: _____

What did I get done today?

_____

_____

_____

_____

What am I grateful for?

_____

_____

_____

What are my top 1-3
priorities for tomorrow?

Micro habit tracker

1. _____   ☐ _____

                              ☐ _____
2. _____
                              ☐ _____

3. _____   ☐ _____

Day 3: _____

What did I get done today?

_____

_____

_____

_____

What am I grateful for?

_____

_____

_____

What are my top 1-3 priorities for tomorrow?

Micro habit tracker

1. _____   ☐ _____

                       ☐ _____

2. _____   ☐ _____

                       ☐ _____

3. _____   ☐ _____

Day 4: _____

What did I get done today?

_____

_____

_____

_____

What am I grateful for?

_____

_____

_____

What are my top 1-3 priorities for tomorrow?

1. _____

2. _____

3. _____

Micro habit tracker

☐ _____

☐ _____

☐ _____

☐ _____

Day 5: _____

What did I get done today?

_____

_____

_____

_____

What am I grateful for?

_____

_____

_____

What are my top 1-3 priorities for tomorrow?	Micro habit tracker
1. _____	☐ _____
	☐ _____
2. _____	☐ _____
	☐ _____
3. _____	☐ _____

Day 6: _____

What did I get done today?

_____

_____

_____

_____

What am I grateful for?

_____

_____

_____

What are my top 1-3 priorities for tomorrow?

Micro habit tracker

1. _____   ☐ _____

☐ _____

2. _____   ☐ _____

3. _____   ☐ _____

Day 7: _____

What did I get done today?

_____

_____

_____

_____

What am I grateful for?

_____

_____

_____

What are my top 1-3 priorities for tomorrow?

1. _____

2. _____

3. _____

Micro habit tracker

☐ _____

☐ _____

☐ _____

☐ _____

Week 1 Review

What am I most proud of this week?

_____

_____

_____

What obstacles or resistance did I face? Where can I improve?

_____

_____

_____

_____

_____

How am I tracking toward my 4-week goal? Shade in the progress bar below:

0%   50%   100%

Day 8: _____

What did I get done today?

_____

_____

_____

_____

What am I grateful for?

_____

_____

_____

What are my top 1-3 priorities for tomorrow?

1. _____

2. _____

3. _____

Micro habit tracker

☐ _____

☐ _____

☐ _____

☐ _____

Day 9: _____

What did I get done today?

_____

_____

_____

_____

What am I grateful for?

_____

_____

_____

What are my top 1-3 priorities for tomorrow?	Micro habit tracker
1. _____	☐ _____
2. _____	☐ _____
3. _____	☐ _____
	☐ _____

Day 10: _____

What did I get done today?

_____

_____

_____

_____

What am I grateful for?

_____

_____

_____

What are my top 1-3 priorities for tomorrow?	Micro habit tracker
1. _____	☐ _____
	☐ _____
2. _____	☐ _____
	☐ _____
3. _____	☐ _____

Day 11: _____

What did I get done today?

_____

_____

_____

_____

What am I grateful for?

_____

_____

_____

What are my top 1-3
priorities for tomorrow?

Micro habit tracker

1. _____

☐ _____

☐ _____

2. _____

☐ _____

3. _____

☐ _____

Day 12: _____

What did I get done today?

_____

_____

_____

_____

What am I grateful for?

_____

_____

_____

What are my top 1-3
priorities for tomorrow?

Micro habit tracker

1. _____

2. _____

3. _____

☐ _____

☐ _____

☐ _____

☐ _____

Day 13: _____

What did I get done today?

_____

_____

_____

_____

What am I grateful for?

_____

_____

_____

What are my top 1-3 priorities for tomorrow?

Micro habit tracker

1. _____   ☐ _____

                            ☐ _____
2. _____
                            ☐ _____

3. _____   ☐ _____

Day 14: _____

What did I get done today?

_____

_____

_____

_____

What am I grateful for?

_____

_____

_____

What are my top 1-3 priorities for tomorrow?

1. _____

2. _____

3. _____

Micro habit tracker

☐ _____

☐ _____

☐ _____

☐ _____

Week 2 Review

What am I most proud of this week?

_____

_____

_____

What obstacles or resistance did I face? Where can I improve?

_____

_____

_____

_____

_____

How am I tracking toward my 4-week goal? Shade in the progress bar below:

0%   50%   100%

Day 15: _____

What did I get done today?

_____

_____

_____

_____

What am I grateful for?

_____

_____

_____

What are my top 1-3 priorities for tomorrow?

1. _____

2. _____

3. _____

Micro habit tracker

☐ _____

☐ _____

☐ _____

☐ _____

Day 16: _____

What did I get done today?

_____

_____

_____

_____

What am I grateful for?

_____

_____

_____

What are my top 1-3 priorities for tomorrow?	Micro habit tracker
1. _____	☐ _____
	☐ _____
2. _____	☐ _____
3. _____	☐ _____

Day 17: _____

What did I get done today?

_____

_____

_____

_____

What am I grateful for?

_____

_____

_____

What are my top 1-3 priorities for tomorrow?

1. _____

2. _____

3. _____

Micro habit tracker

☐ _____

☐ _____

☐ _____

☐ _____

Day 18: _____

What did I get done today?

_____

_____

_____

_____

What am I grateful for?

_____

_____

_____

What are my top 1-3
priorities for tomorrow?

Micro habit tracker

1. _____   ☐ _____

☐ _____

2. _____   ☐ _____

☐ _____

3. _____

Day 19: _____

What did I get done today?

_____

_____

_____

_____

What am I grateful for?

_____

_____

_____

What are my top 1-3 priorities for tomorrow?

Micro habit tracker

1. _____   ☐ _____

                     ☐ _____

2. _____   ☐ _____

                     ☐ _____

3. _____   ☐ _____

Day 20: _____

What did I get done today?

_____

_____

_____

_____

What am I grateful for?

_____

_____

_____

What are my top 1-3
priorities for tomorrow?

Micro habit tracker

1. _____

☐ _____

☐ _____

2. _____

☐ _____

3. _____

☐ _____

Day 21: _____

What did I get done today?

_____

_____

_____

_____

What am I grateful for?

_____

_____

_____

What are my top 1-3 priorities for tomorrow?

Micro habit tracker

1. _____   ☐ _____

☐ _____

2. _____   ☐ _____

☐ _____

3. _____   ☐ _____

Week 3 Review

What am I most proud of this week?

_____

_____

_____

What obstacles or resistance did I face? Where can I improve?

_____

_____

_____

_____

_____

How am I tracking toward my 4-week goal? Shade in the progress bar below:

0%   50%   100%

```
┌─────────────────────────────────────────────┐
│                                               │
│                                               │
│                                               │
└─────────────────────────────────────────────┘
```

Day 22: _____

What did I get done today?

_____

_____

_____

_____

What am I grateful for?

_____

_____

_____

What are my top 1-3 priorities for tomorrow?	Micro habit tracker
1. _____	☐ _____
	☐ _____
2. _____	☐ _____
	☐ _____
3. _____	☐ _____

Day 23: _____

What did I get done today?

_____

_____

_____

_____

What am I grateful for?

_____

_____

_____

What are my top 1-3 priorities for tomorrow?	Micro habit tracker
1. _____	☐ _____
2. _____	☐ _____
3. _____	☐ _____
	☐ _____

Day 24: _____

What did I get done today?

_____

_____

_____

_____

What am I grateful for?

_____

_____

_____

What are my top 1-3 priorities for tomorrow?	Micro habit tracker
1. _____	☐ _____
	☐ _____
2. _____	☐ _____
3. _____	☐ _____

Day 25: _____

What did I get done today?

_____

_____

_____

_____

What am I grateful for?

_____

_____

_____

What are my top 1-3 priorities for tomorrow?

Micro habit tracker

1. _____   ☐ _____

☐ _____

2. _____   ☐ _____

☐ _____

3. _____

Day 26: _____

What did I get done today?

_____

_____

_____

_____

What am I grateful for?

_____

_____

_____

What are my top 1-3 priorities for tomorrow?

Micro habit tracker

1. _____   ☐ _____

2. _____   ☐ _____

                      ☐ _____

3. _____   ☐ _____

Day 27: _____

What did I get done today?

_____

_____

_____

_____

What am I grateful for?

_____

_____

_____

What are my top 1-3
priorities for tomorrow?

Micro habit tracker

1. _____

2. _____

3. _____

☐ _____

☐ _____

☐ _____

☐ _____

Day 28: _____

What did I get done today?

_____

_____

_____

_____

What am I grateful for?

_____

_____

_____

What are my top 1-3 priorities for tomorrow?

Micro habit tracker

1. _____   ☐ _____

☐ _____

2. _____   ☐ _____

3. _____   ☐ _____

Week 4 Review

What am I most proud of this week?

_____

_____

_____

What obstacles or resistance did I face? Where can I improve?

_____

_____

_____

_____

_____

How am I tracking toward my 4-week goal? Shade in the progress bar below:

0%   50%   100%

Block 2 Review

Did I accomplish my primary goal?
☐ Yes! ☐ No

If no, why not?

_____

_____

_____

What worked well over the last 4 weeks?

_____

_____

_____

How am I tracking on my KPI metrics?

1. _____

_____

2. _____

_____

3. _____

_____

4. _____

_____

5. _____

_____

Was I able to "move the needle" on any Key Performance
Indicators? Why or why not?

_____

_____

_____

_____

_____

Block 3

My primary goal for the next 4 weeks is …

_____

_____

What are the key supporting tasks I need to get done to make
that goal a reality? Break it down into the smallest actionable
steps.

_____

_____

_____

_____

_____

_____

_____

_____

What 2-4 micro habits will I track over the next 4 weeks?

1. _____

2. _____

3. _____

4. _____

Where will I start? What are my top 1-3 priorities for tomorrow?

1. _____

2. _____

3. _____

Day 1: _____ (fill in the date)

What did I get done today?

_____

_____

_____

_____

What am I grateful for?

_____

_____

_____

What are my top 1-3
priorities for tomorrow?

Micro habit tracker

1. _____

2. _____

3. _____

☐ _____

☐ _____

☐ _____

☐ _____

Day 2: _____

What did I get done today?

_____

_____

_____

_____

What am I grateful for?

_____

_____

_____

What are my top 1-3 priorities for tomorrow?	Micro habit tracker
1. _____	☐ _____
	☐ _____
2. _____	☐ _____
	☐ _____
3. _____	

Day 3: _____

What did I get done today?

_____

_____

_____

_____

What am I grateful for?

_____

_____

_____

What are my top 1-3 priorities for tomorrow?

1. _____

2. _____

3. _____

Micro habit tracker

☐ _____

☐ _____

☐ _____

☐ _____

Day 4: _____

What did I get done today?

_____

_____

_____

_____

What am I grateful for?

_____

_____

_____

What are my top 1-3 priorities for tomorrow?	Micro habit tracker
1. _____	☐ _____
	☐ _____
2. _____	☐ _____
	☐ _____
3. _____	

Day 5: _____

What did I get done today?

_____

_____

_____

_____

What am I grateful for?

_____

_____

_____

What are my top 1-3 priorities for tomorrow?

Micro habit tracker

1. _____   ☐ _____

2. _____   ☐ _____

☐ _____

3. _____   ☐ _____

Day 6: _____

What did I get done today?

_____

_____

_____

_____

What am I grateful for?

_____

_____

_____

What are my top 1-3 priorities for tomorrow?

Micro habit tracker

1. _____

2. _____

3. _____

☐ _____

☐ _____

☐ _____

☐ _____

Day 7: _____

What did I get done today?

_____

_____

_____

_____

What am I grateful for?

_____

_____

_____

What are my top 1-3 priorities for tomorrow?	Micro habit tracker
1. _____	☐ _____
2. _____	☐ _____
	☐ _____
3. _____	☐ _____

Week 1 Review

What am I most proud of this week?

_____

_____

_____

What obstacles or resistance did I face? Where can I improve?

_____

_____

_____

_____

How am I tracking toward my 4-week goal? Shade in the progress bar below:

0%   50%   100%

Day 8: _____

What did I get done today?

_____

_____

_____

_____

What am I grateful for?

_____

_____

_____

What are my top 1-3 priorities for tomorrow?

1. _____

2. _____

3. _____

Micro habit tracker

☐ _____

☐ _____

☐ _____

☐ _____

Day 9: _____

What did I get done today?

_____

_____

_____

_____

What am I grateful for?

_____

_____

_____

What are my top 1-3
priorities for tomorrow?

Micro habit tracker

1. _____

2. _____

3. _____

☐ _____

☐ _____

☐ _____

☐ _____

Day 10: _____

What did I get done today?

_____

_____

_____

_____

What am I grateful for?

_____

_____

_____

What are my top 1-3 priorities for tomorrow?

1. _____

2. _____

3. _____

Micro habit tracker

☐ _____

☐ _____

☐ _____

☐ _____

Day 11: _____

What did I get done today?

_____

_____

_____

_____

What am I grateful for?

_____

_____

_____

What are my top 1-3
priorities for tomorrow?

Micro habit tracker

1. _____

2. _____

3. _____

☐ _____

☐ _____

☐ _____

☐ _____

Day 12: _____

What did I get done today?

_____

_____

_____

_____

What am I grateful for?

_____

_____

_____

What are my top 1-3 priorities for tomorrow?

Micro habit tracker

1. _____

☐ _____

☐ _____

2. _____

☐ _____

3. _____

☐ _____

Day 13: _____

What did I get done today?

_____

_____

_____

_____

What am I grateful for?

_____

_____

_____

What are my top 1-3 priorities for tomorrow?

1. _____

2. _____

3. _____

Micro habit tracker

☐ _____

☐ _____

☐ _____

☐ _____

Day 14: _____

What did I get done today?

_____

_____

_____

_____

What am I grateful for?

_____

_____

_____

What are my top 1-3 priorities for tomorrow?	Micro habit tracker
1. _____	☐ _____
2. _____	☐ _____
	☐ _____
3. _____	☐ _____

Week 2 Review

What am I most proud of this week?

_____

_____

_____

What obstacles or resistance did I face? Where can I improve?

_____

_____

_____

_____

How am I tracking toward my 4-week goal? Shade in the progress bar below:

0%   50%   100%

Day 15: _____

What did I get done today?

_____

_____

_____

_____

What am I grateful for?

_____

_____

_____

What are my top 1-3 priorities for tomorrow?

1. _____

2. _____

3. _____

Micro habit tracker

☐ _____

☐ _____

☐ _____

☐ _____

Day 16: _____

What did I get done today?

_____

_____

_____

_____

What am I grateful for?

_____

_____

_____

What are my top 1-3 priorities for tomorrow?	Micro habit tracker
1. _____	☐ _____
	☐ _____
2. _____	☐ _____
	☐ _____
3. _____	☐ _____

Day 17: _____

What did I get done today?

_____

_____

_____

_____

What am I grateful for?

_____

_____

_____

What are my top 1-3
priorities for tomorrow?

Micro habit tracker

1. _____

☐ _____

☐ _____

2. _____

☐ _____

3. _____

☐ _____

Day 18: _____

What did I get done today?

_____

_____

_____

_____

What am I grateful for?

_____

_____

_____

What are my top 1-3 priorities for tomorrow?	Micro habit tracker
1. _____	☐ _____
	☐ _____
2. _____	☐ _____
	☐ _____
3. _____	☐ _____

Day 19: _____

What did I get done today?

_____

_____

_____

_____

What am I grateful for?

_____

_____

_____

What are my top 1-3 priorities for tomorrow?

1. _____

2. _____

3. _____

Micro habit tracker

☐ _____

☐ _____

☐ _____

☐ _____

Day 20: _____

What did I get done today?

_____

_____

_____

_____

What am I grateful for?

_____

_____

_____

What are my top 1-3
priorities for tomorrow?

Micro habit tracker

1. _____

☐ _____

☐ _____

2. _____

☐ _____

3. _____

☐ _____

Day 21: _____

What did I get done today?

_____

_____

_____

_____

What am I grateful for?

_____

_____

_____

What are my top 1-3 priorities for tomorrow?	Micro habit tracker
1. _____	☐ _____
	☐ _____
2. _____	☐ _____
	☐ _____
3. _____	☐ _____

Week 3 Review

What am I most proud of this week?

_____

_____

_____

What obstacles or resistance did I face? Where can I improve?

_____

_____

_____

_____

_____

How am I tracking toward my 4-week goal? Shade in the progress bar below:

0%   50%   100%

Day 22: _____

What did I get done today?

_____

_____

_____

_____

What am I grateful for?

_____

_____

_____

What are my top 1-3 priorities for tomorrow?

Micro habit tracker

1. _____

2. _____

3. _____

☐ _____

☐ _____

☐ _____

☐ _____

Day 23: _____

What did I get done today?

_____

_____

_____

_____

What am I grateful for?

_____

_____

_____

What are my top 1-3 priorities for tomorrow?	Micro habit tracker
1. _____	☐ _____
	☐ _____
2. _____	☐ _____
	☐ _____
3. _____	

Day 24: _____

What did I get done today?

_____

_____

_____

_____

What am I grateful for?

_____

_____

_____

What are my top 1-3
priorities for tomorrow?

Micro habit tracker

1. _____

2. _____

3. _____

☐ _____

☐ _____

☐ _____

☐ _____

Day 25: _____

What did I get done today?

_____

_____

_____

_____

What am I grateful for?

_____

_____

_____

What are my top 1-3 priorities for tomorrow?

1. _____

2. _____

3. _____

Micro habit tracker

☐ _____

☐ _____

☐ _____

☐ _____

Day 26: _____

What did I get done today?

_____

_____

_____

_____

What am I grateful for?

_____

_____

_____

What are my top 1-3 priorities for tomorrow?

1. _____

2. _____

3. _____

Micro habit tracker

☐ _____

☐ _____

☐ _____

☐ _____

Day 27: _____

What did I get done today?

_____

_____

_____

_____

What am I grateful for?

_____

_____

_____

What are my top 1-3
priorities for tomorrow?

Micro habit tracker

1. _____

2. _____

3. _____

☐ _____

☐ _____

☐ _____

☐ _____

Day 28: _____

What did I get done today?

_____

_____

_____

_____

What am I grateful for?

_____

_____

_____

What are my top 1-3 priorities for tomorrow?

1. _____

2. _____

3. _____

Micro habit tracker

☐ _____

☐ _____

☐ _____

☐ _____

Week 4 Review

What am I most proud of this week?

_____

_____

_____

What obstacles or resistance did I face? Where can I improve?

_____

_____

_____

_____

_____

How am I tracking toward my 4-week goal? Shade in the progress bar below:

0%   50%   100%

Block 3 Review

Did I accomplish my primary goal?
☐ Yes!   ☐ No

If no, why not?

_____

_____

_____

What worked well over the last 4 weeks?

_____

_____

_____

How am I tracking on my KPI metrics?

1. _____

_____

2. _____

_____

3. _____

_____

4. _____

_____

5. _____

_____

Was I able to "move the needle" on any Key Performance
Indicators? Why or why not?

_____

_____

_____

_____

_____

Block 4

My primary goal for the next 4 weeks is ...

_____

_____

What are the key supporting tasks I need to get done to make
that goal a reality? Break it down into the smallest actionable
steps.

_____

_____

_____

_____

_____

_____

_____

_____

What 2-4 micro habits will I track over the next 4 weeks?

1. _____

2. _____

3. _____

4. _____

Where will I start? What are my top 1-3 priorities for tomorrow?

1. _____

2. _____

3. _____

Day 1: _____ (fill in the date)

What did I get done today?

_____

_____

_____

_____

What am I grateful for?

_____

_____

_____

What are my top 1-3 priorities for tomorrow?

Micro habit tracker

1. _____   ☐ _____

2. _____   ☐ _____

                            ☐ _____

3. _____   ☐ _____

Day 2: _____

What did I get done today?

_____

_____

_____

_____

What am I grateful for?

_____

_____

_____

What are my top 1-3 priorities for tomorrow?

Micro habit tracker

1. _____   ☐ _____

   ☐ _____

2. _____   ☐ _____

3. _____   ☐ _____

Day 3: _____

What did I get done today?

_____

_____

_____

_____

What am I grateful for?

_____

_____

_____

What are my top 1-3 priorities for tomorrow?

Micro habit tracker

1. _____   ☐ _____

                       ☐ _____

2. _____   ☐ _____

                       ☐ _____

3. _____   ☐ _____

Day 4: _____

What did I get done today?

_____

_____

_____

_____

What am I grateful for?

_____

_____

_____

What are my top 1-3 priorities for tomorrow?

1. _____

2. _____

3. _____

Micro habit tracker

☐ _____

☐ _____

☐ _____

☐ _____

Day 5: _____

What did I get done today?

_____

_____

_____

_____

What am I grateful for?

_____

_____

_____

What are my top 1-3
priorities for tomorrow?

Micro habit tracker

1. _____

☐ _____

☐ _____

2. _____

☐ _____

3. _____

☐ _____

Day 6: _____

What did I get done today?

_____

_____

_____

_____

What am I grateful for?

_____

_____

_____

What are my top 1-3 priorities for tomorrow?	Micro habit tracker
1. _____	☐ _____
	☐ _____
2. _____	☐ _____
	☐ _____
3. _____	☐ _____

Day 7: _____

What did I get done today?

_____

_____

_____

_____

What am I grateful for?

_____

_____

_____

What are my top 1-3 priorities for tomorrow?

Micro habit tracker

1. _____   ☐ _____

                           ☐ _____

2. _____   ☐ _____

3. _____   ☐ _____

Week 1 Review

What am I most proud of this week?

_____

_____

_____

What obstacles or resistance did I face? Where can I improve?

_____

_____

_____

_____

How am I tracking toward my 4-week goal? Shade in the progress bar below:

0%   50%   100%

Day 8: _____

What did I get done today?

_____

_____

_____

_____

What am I grateful for?

_____

_____

_____

What are my top 1-3 priorities for tomorrow?

1. _____

2. _____

3. _____

Micro habit tracker

☐ _____

☐ _____

☐ _____

☐ _____

Day 9: _____

What did I get done today?

_____

_____

_____

_____

What am I grateful for?

_____

_____

_____

What are my top 1-3 priorities for tomorrow?

1. _____

2. _____

3. _____

Micro habit tracker

☐ _____

☐ _____

☐ _____

☐ _____

Day 10: _____

What did I get done today?

_____

_____

_____

_____

What am I grateful for?

_____

_____

_____

What are my top 1-3 priorities for tomorrow?

1. _____

2. _____

3. _____

Micro habit tracker

☐ _____

☐ _____

☐ _____

☐ _____

Day 11: _____

What did I get done today?

_____

_____

_____

_____

What am I grateful for?

_____

_____

_____

What are my top 1-3
priorities for tomorrow?

Micro habit tracker

1. _____   ☐ _____

☐ _____

2. _____   ☐ _____

3. _____   ☐ _____

Day 12: _____

What did I get done today?

_____

_____

_____

_____

What am I grateful for?

_____

_____

_____

What are my top 1-3 priorities for tomorrow?

1. _____

2. _____

3. _____

Micro habit tracker

☐ _____

☐ _____

☐ _____

☐ _____

Day 13: _____

What did I get done today?

_____

_____

_____

_____

What am I grateful for?

_____

_____

_____

What are my top 1-3 priorities for tomorrow?

1. _____

2. _____

3. _____

Micro habit tracker

☐ _____

☐ _____

☐ _____

☐ _____

Day 14: _____

What did I get done today?

_____

_____

_____

_____

What am I grateful for?

_____

_____

_____

What are my top 1-3 priorities for tomorrow?

Micro habit tracker

1. _____

2. _____

3. _____

☐ _____

☐ _____

☐ _____

☐ _____

Week 2 Review

What am I most proud of this week?

_____

_____

_____

What obstacles or resistance did I face? Where can I improve?

_____

_____

_____

_____

How am I tracking toward my 4-week goal? Shade in the progress bar below:

0%   50%   100%

Day 15: _____

What did I get done today?

_____

_____

_____

_____

What am I grateful for?

_____

_____

_____

What are my top 1-3 priorities for tomorrow?

1. _____

2. _____

3. _____

Micro habit tracker

☐ _____

☐ _____

☐ _____

☐ _____

Day 16: _____

What did I get done today?

_____

_____

_____

_____

What am I grateful for?

_____

_____

_____

What are my top 1-3 priorities for tomorrow?	Micro habit tracker

1. _____

2. _____

3. _____

☐ _____
☐ _____
☐ _____
☐ _____

Day 17: _____

What did I get done today?

_____

_____

_____

_____

What am I grateful for?

_____

_____

_____

What are my top 1-3
priorities for tomorrow?

Micro habit tracker

1. _____

2. _____

3. _____

☐ _____

☐ _____

☐ _____

☐ _____

Day 18: _____

What did I get done today?

_____

_____

_____

_____

What am I grateful for?

_____

_____

_____

What are my top 1-3 priorities for tomorrow?

1. _____

2. _____

3. _____

Micro habit tracker

☐ _____

☐ _____

☐ _____

☐ _____

Day 19: _____

What did I get done today?

_____

_____

_____

_____

What am I grateful for?

_____

_____

_____

What are my top 1-3 priorities for tomorrow?

1. _____

2. _____

3. _____

Micro habit tracker

☐ _____

☐ _____

☐ _____

☐ _____

Day 20: _____

What did I get done today?

_____

_____

_____

_____

What am I grateful for?

_____

_____

_____

What are my top 1-3 priorities for tomorrow?	Micro habit tracker
1. _____	☐ _____
	☐ _____
2. _____	☐ _____
3. _____	☐ _____

Day 21: _____

What did I get done today?

_____

_____

_____

_____

What am I grateful for?

_____

_____

_____

What are my top 1-3 priorities for tomorrow?

1. _____

2. _____

3. _____

Micro habit tracker

☐ _____

☐ _____

☐ _____

☐ _____

Week 3 Review

What am I most proud of this week?

_____

_____

_____

What obstacles or resistance did I face? Where can I improve?

_____

_____

_____

_____

How am I tracking toward my 4-week goal? Shade in the progress bar below:

0%   50%   100%

Day 22: _____

What did I get done today?

_____

_____

_____

_____

What am I grateful for?

_____

_____

_____

What are my top 1-3
priorities for tomorrow?

Micro habit tracker

1. _____   ☐ _____

                       ☐ _____

2. _____   ☐ _____

                       ☐ _____

3. _____

Day 23: _____

What did I get done today?

_____

_____

_____

_____

What am I grateful for?

_____

_____

_____

What are my top 1-3 priorities for tomorrow?	Micro habit tracker
1. _____	☐ _____
	☐ _____
2. _____	☐ _____
3. _____	☐ _____

Day 24: _____

What did I get done today?

_____

_____

_____

_____

What am I grateful for?

_____

_____

_____

What are my top 1-3 priorities for tomorrow?

1. _____

2. _____

3. _____

Micro habit tracker

☐ _____

☐ _____

☐ _____

☐ _____

Day 25: _____

What did I get done today?

_____

_____

_____

_____

What am I grateful for?

_____

_____

_____

What are my top 1-3 priorities for tomorrow?

1. _____

2. _____

3. _____

Micro habit tracker

☐ _____

☐ _____

☐ _____

☐ _____

Day 26: _____

What did I get done today?

_____

_____

_____

_____

What am I grateful for?

_____

_____

_____

What are my top 1-3
priorities for tomorrow?

Micro habit tracker

1. _____

2. _____

3. _____

☐ _____

☐ _____

☐ _____

☐ _____

Day 27: _____

What did I get done today?

_____

_____

_____

_____

What am I grateful for?

_____

_____

_____

What are my top 1-3 priorities for tomorrow?	Micro habit tracker

1. _____

2. _____

3. _____

☐ _____
☐ _____
☐ _____
☐ _____

Day 28: _____

What did I get done today?

_____

_____

_____

_____

What am I grateful for?

_____

_____

_____

What are my top 1-3 priorities for tomorrow?

1. _____

2. _____

3. _____

Micro habit tracker

☐ _____

☐ _____

☐ _____

☐ _____

Week 4 Review

What am I most proud of this week?

_____

_____

_____

What obstacles or resistance did I face? Where can I improve?

_____

_____

_____

_____

_____

How am I tracking toward my 4-week goal? Shade in the progress bar below:

0%   50%   100%

Block 4 Review

Did I accomplish my primary goal?
☐ Yes!   ☐ No

If no, why not?

_____

_____

_____

What worked well over the last 4 weeks?

_____

_____

_____

How am I tracking on my KPI metrics?

1. _____

_____

2. _____

_____

3. _____

_____

4. _____

_____

5. _____

_____

Was I able to "move the needle" on any Key Performance Indicators? Why or why not?

_____

_____

_____

_____

_____

Final Thoughts: The Journey is the Destination

As a kid, I wasn't much into *Star Trek*, but I was fascinated by the idea of teleportation.

Beam me up!

It's so elegantly efficient; I mean, who wouldn't want to skip all the transit time and instead just instantly arrive where you need to go?

I was all about the destination, and would have been happy skipping the journey entirely.

Are we there yet?

It's taken me a long time to realize this, but **there is no "there."**

The journey *is* the destination.

We've been conditioned to strive toward a number of destinations in our lives:

- Finish high school.
- Graduate from college.
- Get a job.
- Get married.
- Buy a house.
- Start a family.
- Go on vacation.
- Start a business.

- Lose weight.
- Quit your job.
- Retire.

But you know what we find each time we get "there"?

More journey.

In mountain climbing, we call that a false summit.

Even retirement. Every destination—every single one—is greeted with the same question: **"now what?"**

(Only one destination is certain, and it's universal across all ages, races, and nationalities. It's that pesky issue that—not to get too morbid here—ALL our journeys have a 100% mortality rate.)

So what does this have to do with entrepreneurship and productivity?

A lot!

This isn't a call to stop and smell the roses, but it is a reminder that no matter where you are today in terms of your business, you're on the path. You're making progress; moving forward.

Even the people who've supposedly "arrived" **don't see it that way,** so you shouldn't either.

If you're a long-time listener of the Entrepreneur on Fire podcast, you might recall that host John Lee Dumas used to ask his guests if they'd had **"an I've 'made it' moment."**

But he stopped asking it because nearly every answer was the same:

"Kinda ... not really. I've had some success, but I still have work to do."

Now, I'm all for setting goals. After all, if you don't know where you're going, how are you going to know how to get there?

But I'm coming to see them more as **milestones rather than endpoints,** because the journey doesn't stop there.

And here's the best part: since the journey *is* the destination, you get to choose your own adventure every day and embrace it as a destination on its own.

After all, your whole life has led you to this day.

Reframed through that lens, challenges and barriers that stand in your way become little **mini-quests to conquer.** That doesn't mean it's always going to be easy or fun (it's not), but it does allow you to be proactive and positive about the journey.

Have you heard this quote from Jon Acuff?

"Don't compare your beginning to someone else's middle."

There's a reason he didn't say "someone else's finish line." Because it's *all* middle.

Keep the Conversation Going

If you'd like to join a supportive and active community of other entrepreneurs and side hustlers, please join the free Side Hustle Nation Facebook group:

SideHustleNation.com/fb

You'll be able to ask questions, help others on their journey, and share your victories along the way.

Liked the Journal?

If you liked this journal, it would mean the world to me if you took a moment to leave an honest review on Amazon. Thank you!

You can also grab your next copy at ProgressJournal.net.

Claim Your Free Bonuses

In the spirit of improving not just your productivity, but your overall effectiveness, I put together an exclusive bonus package for users of *The Progress Journal.*

1. The Productivity Tip Sheet

I asked some of my most successful entrepreneurial friends for their favorite productivity tips and tricks.

The result is this Tip Sheet.

I don't expect you to try all of these—especially not all at once—but use the suggestions on this list to re-energize and re-focus.

2. The Digital Progress Journal

Several readers requested a digital version of the journal to use with their tablet and stylus. If you're embracing a paperless lifestyle, this one is for you.

Plus, it includes 2 extra time blocks free.

Grab them both free here:

ProgressJournal.net/bonus

About the Author

Nick Loper is an online entrepreneur and lifelong student in the game of business. He lives in Northern California with his wife Bryn, two sons, and a lovable giant Shih-Tzu called Mochi.

On a typical day you can find him working on his latest business idea, recording another episode of the award-winning Side Hustle Show podcast, rooting for the Huskies, or skiing the Sierra pow.

Nick has witnessed the power of tracking his progress on meaningful projects many times over, until it finally hit him that he should write a book about it.

As you can probably tell from the book, he gets really excited about this stuff and wants to help others find success online.

Want to know more?

Drop by and check out his blog and podcast at SideHustleNation.com, a growing resource and community for aspiring and part-time entrepreneurs.

Connect with fellow side hustlers to share wins, get feedback, and support each in the free Facebook group:

SideHustleNation.com/fb

Do you have a *Progress Journal* success story to share? Get in touch (nick@sidehustlenation.com)!

Also by Nick

Nick is also the author of:

Buy Buttons: The Fast-Track Strategy to Make Extra Money and Start a Business in Your Spare Time

The Side Hustle Path: 10 Proven Ways to Make Money Outside of Your Day Job (4-part series)

The Small Business Website Checklist: A 51-Point Guide to Build Your Online Presence The Smart Way

Virtual Assistant Assistant: The Ultimate Guide to Finding, Hiring, and Working with Virtual Assistants

Work Smarter: 500+ Online Resources Today's Top Entrepreneurs Use to Increase Productivity and Achieve Their Goals

Made in the USA
Las Vegas, NV
25 November 2023